Anonymous

The Paraguayan question

The alliance between Brazil, the Argentine Confederation and Uruguay

versus the dictator of Paraguay

Anonymous

The Paraguayan question
The alliance between Brazil, the Argentine Confederation and Uruguay versus the dictator of Paraguay

ISBN/EAN: 9783337197414

Printed in Europe, USA, Canada, Australia, Japan

Cover: Foto ©Suzi / pixelio.de

More available books at **www.hansebooks.com**

THE PARAGUAYAN QUESTION.

THE ALLIANCE

BETWEEN

BRAZIL, THE ARGENTINE CONFEDERATION AND URUGUAY,

VERSUS

THE DICTATOR OF PARAGUAY.

CLAIMS OF THE REPUBLICS OF PERU AND BOLIVIA
IN REGARD TO THIS ALLIANCE.

NEW YORK:
HALLET & BREEN, PRINTERS, 58 & 60 FULTON STREET.
1866.

BRAZIL,

THE STATES OF LA PLATA

AND PARAGUAY.

ORIGIN AND CAUSES OF THE WAR BETWEEN THOSE SOUTH
AMERICAN STATES AND PARAGUAY.

The questions of a country, in relation to its international rights, are seldom well understood, if they do not affect the general interests, and are but of a secondary importance to the great Powers in the working of the foreign policy which most immediately concerns them.

It is not, then, strange that certain organs of the Press in the United States should not rightly understand the war carried on by Brazil, the Argentine Republic, and Uruguay against the present Dictator of Paraguay; the motives which led those three American States to combine and unite in an alliance, offensive and defensive, to repel a common enemy; and the end which they proposed to reach by means of this alliance.

It is necessary to go back to the origin of the struggle, and examine the course of events, to explain the present state of affairs, and the new developments which, with the help of Divine Providence, and for the good of mankind, are now taking place in that section of South America.

Brazil and the Argentine and Uruguay Republics formed an Alliance, on the 27th of August, 1828, to remove all and any causes of difficulty in their international relations.

The articles of this agreement were confirmed and ratified

in the treaties entered into between Brazil and the aforesaid republics on the 12th of October, 1851; and in the treaty of ,friendly relations, commerce, and navigation of 7th of March, 1856, between the Empire and the Argentine Confederation.

The violation of the first-named treaty by the iron dictatorship of General Don Juan Manuel Rosas, gave occasion for the other treaties and the principles subsequently adopted in 1859, to secure the entire and absolute independence and sovereignty of the Oriental ' Republic of Uruguay in her foreign relations.

Said treaties establish the equilibrium of the La Plata countries, which, according to the declaration of General Lopez, present Dictator of Paraguay, was endangered on the 30th August, 1864, by the mere fact that the Government of Brazil, with the assent of its other ally, demanded just satisfaction from the Government illegally in power at that time in Uruguay, for the atrocious offences committed against Brazilian subjects there residing, in disregard and in open violation of the existing treaties.

The incident to which we have just alluded, and which interrupted for a while the intimate and friendly relations between the Empire and the Oriental Republic of Uruguay, ended, however, very satisfactorily, by the agreement signed in Montevideo on the 20th February, 1865, by which the alliance between Brazil and the States of La Plata became still more firmly established.

This question solely affected the States already mentioned, and did not affect the security or the interests of the Republic of Paraguay, which was, in fact, so remote from the theatre of events, and with which the Empire was in perfect peace.

In the meantime, without the least provocation and without any previous declaration of war, and in truth, caring nought for the equilibrium of those States, General Lopez took this difficulty as a pretext for ordering the treacherous detention, at Assumption, of a Brazilian steamer, on board of which was the President entrusted by the Imperial Government with the administration of the remote and important Brazilian Province of Matto-Grosso ; and, also, used it to disguise his real intentions of surprising that Province by invasion.

The manifesto addressed on the 26th of January of last year by the Brazilian Government, through its Minister in Buenos Ayres, to the Foreign Powers, made evident how unjust and unheard of was this audacious proceeding on the part of the Government of Paraguay.

To Brazil it is that Paraguay was indebted for the recognition of her independence by several European and American Governments, at a time when her political existence was seriously threatened by the dictatorship of General Rosas, governor of the Argentine Provinces.

Many a time since the independence of Paraguay was established, has Brazil had cause to demand reparation for the continued offences committed against her in despite of the most solemn treaties ; she has, nevertheless, always acted with the greatest moderation, ever willing to enter into new agreements, to settle by friendly means the question of boundaries, and also the free navigation of the entire river from the La Plata to the upper Paraguay.

The last treaty upon these questions is dated February 28th, 1858.

From that date to the year 1864, there was a cessation of difficulties between the two countries, and just as Brazil was flattered with the idea that the two countries were becoming more united, and their mutual relations more firm, Paraguay, during that term of tranquility, was lying in wait for the opportunity of invading and perpetrating all manner of atrocities against the neighboring Province of Matto-Grosso, to decide in this summary manner the question of boundaries about which it had never been possible to come to an agreement, on account of the exaggerated demands of its government, as is proved by all the negociations since the year 1853.

The world is still horrified by the acts of barbarity perpetrated in that Province by order of the Dictator of Paraguay, without any consideration to age, sex, or helplessness; entire populations being shot down like wild beasts in the rivers and forests as they fled from the fury of the enemy.

Are not these more than sufficient causes to justify Brazil in a war which she neither sought nor provoked but accepted only to recover her rights, to drive the enemy from her country, and to avenge the innocent blood of her children sacrificed to the whim of the most ambitious of tyrants.

Exercising her legitimate rights, Brazil then commenced hostilities by blockading the ports and the communications of Paraguay. These hostilities could not be extended through the territory on the left bank of the river Parana, without permission from the Argentine Republic, and this permission was refused.

This permission was likewise refused when asked by Paraguay, upon which the government of that State, disregarding all international rights, invaded the territory in question, capturing, also, two Argentine steamers, and occupying, on the 13th April of last year, the capital of the Province of Corrientes and its surroundings, which then became the theatre of the same outrages that had before been committed in the Brazilian territory.

These acts of unexpected hostility compelled the Argentine Government, in its turn, to accept the war thus commenced against her without warning, and without the least provocation on her part, and thus the interests of Brazil and of the Argentine Republic became identified; both countries had to avenge the wrongs and offences committed against their sovereignty and independence; and by a chain of unforeseen circumstances both were united in that glorious campaign whose object is the triumph of civilization against barbarism, and whose standard is the great cause of humanity.

The concurrence of General Don Venancio Flores is explained by his former alliance with the Governments of Brazil and the Argentine Republic, and by the unwarranted interference of the Dictator of Paraguay in the internal affairs of the Oriental Republic.

TREATY OF ALLIANCE OF MAY 1ST, 1865.

The three Governments, having the same causes of complaint and the same interests to defend, could not do otherwise than unite in their own defense; and to that end, on the 1st of May, 1865, they entered into a treaty of alliance, which was already in existence *de facto*, owing to the acts of Dictator Lopez.

Annexed to the treaty is a protocol of the same date, which serves as its complement.

The public has not yet been put in possession of certain secret notes, which, without doubt, will explain fully, the views and intentions of the high contracting parties at the time of signing the said treaty.

We believe that the most fastidious person will be entirely satisfied with the context of the said treaty.

As the treaty to which we allude has already been published, either through oversight or intentionally—it now matters little which—we here transcribe literally the main conditions, as they are known to the public, to the end that they be better understood :

"ART. 6.—The allies solemnly bind themselves not to lay down their arms unless by common consent, nor until they have overturned the actual government of Paraguay [*i. e.* Lopez]; neither shall they separately treat of nor sign any treaty of peace, truce, armistice or agreement, whatever, to end or suspend the war, except it be mutually agreed to.

ART. 7.—As the war is not waged against the people of Paraguay, but against its government, the allies may admit into a Paraguayan legion all the citizens of that nation who may wish to aid in the overthrow of said government, and will furnish them with whatever they may need, in the form and under the conditions that shall be agreed upon.

ART. 8.—The allies bind themselves to respect the independence, sovereignty and territorial integrity of the republic of Paraguay. In consequence, the people of Paraguay shall be enabled to choose whatever government and institutions may suit them, without having to submit, as a result of the war, to incorporation with any of the allies or having to accept the protectorate of any of them.

ART. 9.—The independence, sovereignity and territorial integrity of the republic of Paraguay shall, in accordance with the preceding article, be guaranteed collectively by the high contracting parties for the term of five years.

ART. 10.—It is agreed between the high contracting parties that the exemptions, privileges or concessions which they may obtain from the government of Paraguay shall be common to them all—gratuitously, should they be so obtained, and upon common conditions, should they be gotten conditionally.

ART. 11.—After the present government of Paraguay shall have been overthrown, the allies shall proceed to make the necessary arrangements with the newly constituted authority in order to secure the free navigation of the rivers Parana and Paraguay, so that the laws or regulations of said republic may not obstruct, impede or tax the transit across, or navigation along, said rivers by the merchant or war vessels of the allied States bound to points within their respective territories, or within territory which may not belong to Paraguay; and they shall require proper guarantees to secure the effectiveness of such arrangements, but on condition that such arrangements concerning river policy—whether as regards the aforementioned rivers' or the Uruguay as well—shall be drawn up in common accord between the allies and whatever other littoral States may, within the period agreed upon by the allies, accept the invitation that may be extended to them.

ART. 12.—The allies reserve to themselves the right of concerting the most suitable measures to guarantee peace with the republic of Paraguay after the overthrow of its present government.

ART. 13.—The allies will, at the proper time, name the plenipotentiaries who shall represent them in conference to make whatever agreements, conventions or treaties may be necessary with the new government that shall be established in Paraguay.

ART. 14.—The allies shall exact from said government payment for the expenses caused by this war—a war which has been forced upon them; and also reparation and indemnification for the injuries and wrongs done to their public as well as to their private property, and to the persons of their citizens previous to any express declaration of war; likewise for the injuries and wrongs caused subsequently, in violation of the principles that govern in the laws of war.

The Oriental Republic of Uruguay shall, moreover, exact an indemnity proportionate to the injuries and wrongs which the government of Paraguay has done her in this war, into which it compelled her to enter for the defence of her rights threatened by said government.

ART. 15.—By a special agreement it will be provided for the manner and form of the settlements to be made under the preceding article.

ART. 16.—In order to avoid the discussions and wars which arise out of questions relating to territorial boundaries, it is agreed that the allies shall require of the government of Paraguay to make a special treaty with each one to define their respective boundaries on the following bases :

The Argentine Republic shall be separated from the Republic of Paraguay by the rivers Parana and Paraguay, up to the point where said rivers touch Brazilian soil, such points, in the case of the Paraguay river, being on its right bank at the Bahia Negra.

The Empire of Brazil shall be separated from the Republic of Paraguay, on the side of the Parana, by the first river below the falls called the Seven Cataracts, which, according the new map of Manchez, is the Ygurey, running the line from the mouth of the said river Ygurey, along its whole course to its source. On the left bank of the river Paraguay it shall be separated by the river Apa, from its mouth to its source. In the interior they shall be separated by the Maracajú range of mountains, the eastern slopes of which belong to Brazil, and the western to Paraguay, between the two points at which the shortest straight lines can be drawn respectively from the said range to the sources of the Apa and Ygurey.

ART. 17.—The allies mutually guarantee to each other the faithful fulfilment of the agreements, conventions and treaties that it may be necessary to make with the government that is to be established in Paraguay, in accordance with the stipulations of the present treaty of alliance, which shall remain in full force and vigor until those stipulations be respected and fulfilled by the Republic of Paraguay.

In order to obtain this result they agree that, in case one of the higher contracting parties fails to obtain from the government of Paraguay the fulfilment of its agreement, or that the latter government attempt to annul the stipulations agreed to with the allies, the others shall actively use their efforts to obtain, their fulfilment. Should these be useless, the allies shall join together all their means to render effective the stipulations made with them.

ART. 18.—This treaty shall remain a secret until the principal object of the alliance be obtained.

PROTOCOL.

Their Excellencies the plenipotentiaries of the Argentine Republic, of the Oriental republic of Uruguay, and of his Majesty the Emperor of Brazil, having convened in the office of Foreign Affairs, have agreed :

1st, That in execution of the Treaty of Alliance of this date, the fortifications of Humaita shall be demolished; and it shall not be permitted to erect others of a like nature that might impede the faithful execution of said treaty.

2nd. That, it being one of the necessary measures to guarantee a peace with the government which shall be established in Paraguay, that there be left in Paraguay neither arms nor munitions of war; such as may be found there shall be divided in equal parts among the allies.

3rd. That the trophies or booty which may be taken from the enemy shall be divided among the allies capturing the same.

4th. That the commanders of the allied armies shall concert the measures necessary to carry into effect what is herein stipulated."

In the stipulations above referred to, there is nothing to be wondered at; it is in the interest of all American nationalities that these stipulations should be fully carried out.

By assisting the Paraguayan people to shake off the tyrant's yoke, the allies open to them the way to progress and civilization.

Raising them from slavery, the Allies substitute for the present brutalizing system of servitude, the aspirations of a free people.

There is no design against the independence and sovereignty of Paraguay, the only end being to overthrow a tyrant, whose political existence is inconsistent with the enlightenment of the age.

The end of the Allies is only to restore the nationality of another American people, giving them the peace and security constantly threatened by the treachery which is the basis of the traditional policy of the present governor of that republic.

Neither is there any design of forcing on that people a new government, or of interfering with any form by which they may prefer to be governed.

The independence, integrity, and sovereignty of the Paraguayan people is collectively guaranteed to them in all its plenitude ; it is not allowed to any of the Allies to exercise the least Protectorate over the Republic as a result of the war.

The Allies, far from designing to usurp territories that do not rightfully belong to them, are only defending their own rights, as we shall hereafter show.

ANALOGY WITH THE TREATY OF THE QUADRUPLE ALLIANCE BETWEEN CHILI, PERU, BOLIVIA, AND ECUADOR, OF 23D JANUARY, 1865.

There is a remarkable coincidence between the clauses of Article 8 of the treaty of May 1st, 1865, with the clause of Article 2 of the treaty of the quadruple alliance contracted by Chili, Peru, Bolivia, and Ecuador, on the 23d of January of the same year.

The end of the high contracting parties in this last-named treaty was to provide for their exterior security, to maintain peace among themselves, and to promote other common interests.

We cannot here enter into the consideration of the policy which dictated the agreements of the Allies; nor discuss the question whether these are the best means of making closer the ties of friendship and good understanding between the different nations and governments, with the view of avoiding all future war.

The alliance was entered into to the end that it should have its due effect, especially in the cases foreseen in the following paragraphs :

" 1st. Should any design be formed to deprive one of the high contracting parties of part of its territory, with the purpose of holding it, or ceding it to another power.

2d. Should its form of government, its constitution and political institutions be annulled or altered.

3rd. Should any of the said contracting parties be compelled to a protectorate, sale or cession of its territory, or should any other acts be committed against its sovereignty and independence."

This treaty, however, can have no application to the present war provoked and carried on by Paraguay against Brazil and the Republics of La Plata, which on their part only repel an unjust aggression.

The Republic of Paraguay, so far as is known, took no part in this agreement, and consequently can have no part in the rights and obligations proceeding therefrom.

And even though Lopez should have taken part in it, his cause would be defeated by Article 1st., and by the spirit of the alliance of 1st May, which tends expressly to put down any acts of ambition and usurpation on the part of any of the American Powers which shall interrupt that peace which it is so important to maintain on this Continent, to secure its social improvement, to strengthen its institutions, and to place it in an advantageous position against any foreign aggression.

PRECEDENT THAT JUSTIFIES THE CONDUCT OF THE ALLIES.

The treaty of the 1st May, which is attracting so much attention in the Republics of the Pacific, is a repetition of the one entered into on the 21st of November, 1851, between Brazil, some of the Argentine Provinces, and the Oriental Republic of Uruguay, against the Governor of Buenos Ayres, that government being also inconsistent with the peace, security and welfare of the allies.

The allies solemnly declare in the 1st Article of that treaty, that they had no intention of making war on the Argentine Confederation, or of interfering in any way with the liberty of the people in the exercise of the sovereign rights derived from their laws and treaties, and from the perfect independence of the Nation.

The only end they had in view was to liberate the Argentine people from the oppression which they suffered, under the tyrannical sway of the governor, Don Juan Manuel Rosas, and enable them to adopt such form of government as they should deem conducive to their own interests, peace and friendship towards the neighboring States, and placing themselves on a sure basis, by establishing with them political and friendly relations, which are so essential for their mutual progress and improvement.

It will be well, here, to let our attention dwell on the broad and generous policy which the allies acted upon at that time, and which they are now endeavoring to unfold in the war forced upon them by the Paraguayan Republic.

Rosas, the Governor of Buenos Ayres, interposed every kind of difficulty to the free navigation of the affluents of the river La Plata.

It was of the utmost importance to make the island of Martin Garcia neutral, as by its situation at the mouth of the rivers Parana and Uruguay, it commands, and could obstruct, if not forbid, the said navigation.

By the treaties of the 12th of October, 1851, and by 7th of March, 1856, concluded after the fall of General Rosas, between Brazil and the Oriental and Argentine Republics, that island was made neutral, and the free navigation guaranteed to the contracting parties.

The navigation of the rivers Parana and Paraguay has always been subjected to the same difficulties by the Government of Paraguay, in that part of the said rivers belonging to it.

By article 11 of the treaty of the 1st May, 1865, the free navigation of these rivers has been also guaranteed in such manner that no regulations or laws of Paraguay shall be able to hinder, obstruct, or make onerous the passage by these waters.

The guarantee indispensably needed for the said free navigation is the destruction of the fortress of Humaita.

Therefore the destruction of that fortress was determined on, in the protocol of the same date.

The object of this stipulation, and of others of a like nature, was also to put it out of the power of Paraguay to repeat her aggressions against the allies whose territory adjoined hers.

Modern history presents several instances where similar means have been taken to secure peace.

As for the independence and sovereignty of the republic, they are not endangered in the least, being, on the contrary, expressly guaranteed by the allies collectively, in each and all of their treaties and agreements.

PREJUDICES AGAINST THE POLICY OF BRAZIL.

The Dictator Lopez is making it appear through the press of Europe and America that, in the war undertaken by him, his only object is to oppose the encroachments of Brazil.

These subtle falsehoods, unfortunately, find believers in some of the South American States, where the least incident serves to revive the ancient rivalries inherited from their respective mother countries.

Whenever any question of boundaries is raised, the artful pretensions of Azara are brought up, and, no allowance being made for the natural growth and development which has altered the boundaries once defined by certain old, and now worthless, provisional treaties, it is said that the people of Brazil, animated by the spirit of conquest of their ancestors, pretend to extend their dominions beyond the limits determined by their *uti possedetis* at the time of their independence from Portugal, or by treaties where that title is not prevailing.

All the responsibility of a struggle is thus thrown upon a government which has always striven to be on good terms with its neighbors, has ever been foremost in the desire to have the boundary question settled peacefully by diplomatic arrangements, and has invariably proceeded in its negociations with the utmost moderation, and in the most conciliatory spirit.

All manner of reproaches are now heaped upon Brazil, while she it was who first opened her rivers to all her neighbors, upon the most liberal principles.

Hence it is that we see in some of the American journals the most erroneous opinions with regard to the views and designs of Brazil in entering into the treaty of the 1st of May with the Argentine Republic and Uruguay.

We find these questions thus resolved, through the distrust excited in the small American States by the monarchical form of Government by which Brazil is ruled, although in fact her institutions are more essentially American than are those of many of those nations.

Is there in the world a more liberal constitution, greater freedom of discussion, a freer Press, or a more perfect general liberty?

Even as regards liberty of conscience, the character of the Brazilian people give to it the fullest amplitude, notwithstanding that the religion of the State is established by the Constitution.

Let us, however, put aside the subject of these rivalries, knowing that some day they will be finally destroyed, and let us pass on to a few considerations:

When a country is blest with free institutions, what matters it to the community of nations whether the chief of that country is a monarch or a temporary president?

The grand requisite in a government, in whatever form it may exist, is that it shall be the true representative of the people, protecting the rights of individuals, and having for its rule of conduct the spirit of justice and equality; in a word, the government should be suited to the age.

Giving to his government the title of Republic, Rosas called himself the restorer of the laws. The title of Republican is also assumed by Lopez, who inflames the superstition of his people by the promise of a speedy resurrection if they sacrifice their lives at his command, and imperils their souls by urging them on to crime.

What does the political and commercial world gain from the existence of despots of this kind, who crush out all freedom in the nationality of their countries, and seek to perpetuate therein a state of barbarism by cutting it off from contact with civilized nations?

Brazil, the Argentine Republic, and Uruguay won the

applause of all Christendom by driving from Buenos Ayres
the founder of the *mashorca* (wholesale hanging), and the
same applause will be bestowed on them if, firmly persever-
ing in their noble mission, they succeed in driving from
Asuncion its ferocious despot.

BASIS FOR SETTLING THE QUESTION OF BOUNDARIES WITH THE EMPIRE OF BRAZIL.

To obviate the difficulties and wars constantly springing
from the questions of boundaries, it was determined by Art.
XVI. of the treaty of the triple alliance that the allies should
oblige the Government of Paraguay to enter into special
treaties with each of the Governments severally, upon a certain basis.

The boundaries determined upon that basis are the same
which were proposed by Brazil, in 1856, in the conferences
between the plenipotentiaries of both countries, as appears
from the respective protocols.

The Government of Paraguay claimed that the bounda-
ries of the two countries ought to be, on the side of the
Parana, the River Ivinheima; and on the side of the Para-
guay, the River Blanco, whose course lies to the north of the
Apa, these two rivers being united by the mountains of
Maracaju or Amambahy.

The Government of the Empire, on the other side, claimed
that the boundary ought to be by the River Iguatemy and
by the Apa, and the mountain of Maracaju which divides
the waters of the Parana from those of the Paraguay.

To the allegations and specious arguments by which the
Government of Paraguay urged its exaggerated claims, the
Government of Brazil opposed the testimony of the treaties
of 1750 and 1777, the agreements entered into in 1778 by
the mother countries, and by its well-established possessions
of the disputed territories.

The term appointed for the renewal of the negociations
expired on the 6th of April, 1862.

Notwithstanding the most ardent wishes of the Empire, unavoidable circumstances rendered it impossible to continue the discussion of this important subject.

The boundaries of the Iguatemy river, a little above the Igurey, was one of the concessions made by Brazil, solely in behalf of peace.

Now, however, Brazil being forced to the unjust war thrust upon her by the Republic of Paraguay, and the solution of the question being removed from the Pacific ground on which the Government of Brazil has patiently endeavored to maintain it, it has become necessary for her to insist on the titles which, in default of possession of each of the contending parties, are given in Arts. V. and VI. of the treaty of 1850, and Arts. VIII. and IX. of the treaty of 1777, which can be consulted in all the collections published for the use of those who interest themselves in these barren and complicated questions.

This is the full explanation of the basis upon which the Government of the Empire purposes to settle the question of boundaries now pending with the Republic of Paraguay.

THE BEARING OF THE STIPULATIONS CONCERNING THE QUESTION ALSO PENDING WITH THE REPUBLIC OF BOLIVIA.

The boundary with the Republic of Bolivia will begin at the end of the boundary line proposed to the Republic of Paraguay, that is to say, from *Bahia Negra* to .the North, and not from the mouth of the Apa in latitude 22° 5′, as pretended in 1851.

Bahia Negra, on the right bank of the Paraguay River, was recognized in the negociations that took place in Rio de Janeiro, in 1856, as the boundary between the two countries in that section.

The same recognition was formally set forth in the special protocol drawn up at Asuncion by the respective plenipotentiaries who signed the convention of the 12th of February, 1858, on the true meaning and practical application of the treaty of friendship, navigation and commerce of the 6th of April in that year.

This recognition was not intended to invalidate any right or titles that might be put forth by the Government of Bolivia to the right bank of the Paraguay River, between the parallels of 20°, 21° and 22°, that is to say, to the territory comprised from *Bahia Negra* to opposite the river Apa.

In this matter Brazil acted with the same moderation which it had observed towards Peru, in the negociation of the treaty of boundaries concluded with that Republic.

The Province of Maynas, adjoining the Empire, was recognized as belonging to Peru, on the ground that portions of the territory were actually in possession of the Republic.

The Republics of Ecuador and New Granada also have claims upon that territory, and the rights which both or either might eventually put forward were reserved in the protocal of the negociations, with the proviso, however, that the boundary of Brazil, established on the *uti possedetis* could not be altered.

Mr. Cruz Benavente, Bolivian Chargé d'Affaires at Buenos Ayres, on the 22nd of August, 1852, addressed to the Government of the Argentine Confederation, a protest approved by his Government, against the treaty of navigation and boundaries formed on the 15th of July of that year, between the Republic of Paraguay and the Argentine Confederation, urging the rights of his country.

The protest of the Bolivian agent was based on the assertion that Bolivia extended on the Western bank of the Paraguay River, between 20°, 21° and 22°.

The Argentine Government answered that protest on the 24th of the same month, August, in the following terms :

That the concluding of a treaty with the Government of Paraguay could not in any way interfere with the rights claimed by the Republic of Bolivia.

The Government of Bolivia accepted this declaration as the explanation of the true meaning of Art. IV. of the treaty of boundaries and navigation, and her rights remained undisturbed.

Brazil, while recognizing that she has no right or claims of any kind to the western bank of the Paraguay, to the south of Bahia Negra, cannot make the same declaration concerning the said western bank to the north as far as 16° 23', or unto the boundary line of Jauru.

To obtain such a concession, the Bolivian Government would have to re-establish the old boundaries of the provinces which formed the ancient Viceroyalty of Buenos Ayres, as they are defined in the treaties concluded in the last century by the Kings of Spain and Portugal; and, moreover, it would have to be proven that Brazil was not the only possessor of both the banks of the river in that part.

PRINCIPLES BY WHICH THE TREATIES OF BOUNDARIES ARE TO BE REGULATED BETWEEN BRAZIL AND THE SOUTH AMERICAN REPUBLICS.

The Republics of South America sometimes refer to the treaties of 1750 and 1777, and sometimes consider them null and void. The truth, with regard to the said treaties, is this :

The treaty of the 13th of January, 1750, was annulled by the treaty of the 12th of February, 1761; and after this came the war of 1762, which was terminated by the treaty of Paris of the 10th of February, 1763, things remaining then as they were before. The treaty of the 1st of October, 1777 followed then, and shared the fate of the one of 1750, which it ratified in most of its parts. The uncertainty which sprang up when the boundaries were to be defined, prevented the recognition from having its full effects; and finally, the war of 1801 annulled it for ever, as the treaty of peace signed at Badajoz on the 6th of June of the same year, neither restored it nor ordered that things should return to their state *ante bellum*.

This, however, does not mean that recourse should not be

had to the stipulations of those treaties ás an auxiliary basis
on which to determine what was Portuguese territory, and
what was Spanish territory, and also what were the changes
in the possessions of each nationality in the lapse of time
and the course of events. In places where one of two nations contests the claims of the other, and such claim is not
determined by effective occupation or material proofs of possession, that basis can throw light on the matter, and settle
it at once.

Brazil has an unquestionable right to all the territory in
South America, formerly belonging to Portugal, with the
losses and acquisitions incurred after the treaties of 1750 and
1777; and in like manner the adjoining States, which were
formerly colonies of Spain, own all the territories formerly
iu possession of that nation, saving only the alterations determined by their *uti possedetis*.

Should this basis be rejected or unheeded, the only arbiter
would be force, or the convenience of each country.

Concerning the basis of the claims of the Bolivian Government in the old question of its boundaries with Brazil,
there is nothing in it that has not been already discussed
between the diplomatic agents of the two countries.

There was a time (1838) when the Government of that
republic refused to recognise the treaties of 1750 and 1777,
denying even their existence in the archives of the republic,
and declaring that it had never given to them the formal
consent which would have bound it to observe its stipulations after the transformation of the territories that pre-
viously belonged to the ancient contracting powers. It was
only in 1843 that the republic commenced to insist on the
validity of these treaties ; and in 1858, still taking from
them her title, protested against the military posts established by Brazil at Coimbra, Albuquerque, Corumba, Dourados,
Onças, Lages, Tremedal (Corixa Grande), Cambara, Pe-
derneiras, and Registro de Jaurú.

At all events, it is not possible for Brazil to abandon the

long possession, acquired by succession, in these territories, considered as having belonged to the Spaniards.

The titles held up by Brazil in this complicated question of boundaries are the very ones exhibited in the negociations with the Oriental Republic of Uruguay in 1851; with the Argentine Confederation in 1857; with the Republic of Paraguay on the south since 1843; and with Venezuela on the north, and Peru and New Granada on the west.

Bolivia possesses the insignificant seaport of Cobija, at the mouth of the river Salado, and on that account insists on having a share in the waters of the Paraguay and Amazonas, in the very legitimate interest of having easy egress to the ocean, and thus securing more immediate contact with the commercial world.

It is not the fault of the Empire that the Republic of Bolivia does not yet enjoy all these advantages, as it has offered to her the same facilities of navigation, through the Brazilian rivers, which have already been secured, in the most liberal treaties to Peru and Venezuela, *ad instar* of those entered into with the Republics of La Plata and Paraguay, based on the principles recognized and proclaimed by the Congress of Vienna.

BASIS FOR SETTLING THE QUESTION OF BOUNDARIES WITH THE ARGENTINE REPUBLIC, AND ITS RELATIONS TO THE QUESTIONS ALSO PENDING BETWEEN THAT REPUBLIC AND BOLIVIA.

The principles above referred to as regulators of the boundaries between Brazil and the different South American States, cannot be equally applied to the boundaries separating the different fractions of the ancient Viceroyalties and Captaincies-General into which the Spanish possessions on this continent were divided.

Paraguay separated from the Viceroyalty to which it belonged in 1811, or rather in 1813, when under the rule of

Dictator Francia. Bolivia separated from the Viceroyalty of Peru in 1825.

Since that time, vast uninhabited territories have remained *pro indiviso*, through the want of a solid basis on which to settle their boundaries among the contending parties.

It is the want of this basis which has most contributed to create the international difficulties between the American nations of Spanish origin, which, for the greater part, have never found a satisfactory conclusion.

Such is the position in which the Argentine Republic and Paraguay have found themselves until of late ; nor were the difficulties settled even in 1852, when Paraguay recognized the total separation of Buenos Ayres from the Argentine Republic.

Bolivia lays claim to the territory of the *Gran Chaco*, on the right bank of the Paraguay river; but the discussion of this claim, which has heretofore been held with Paraguay, after the war, will have to be held with the Argentine Republic.

CONCLUSION.

What we have here set forth will suffice to show how groundless were the complaints made by the Government of Bolivia to the Brazilian Government on the 6th of July, and how wrong was the basis of the despatch sent by the Government of Peru to its representative in Buenos Ayres. Of this despatch, we must say that we could hardly believe it genuine, did not we know that diplomacy is, alas! often blinded by ignorance, and misled by the misrepresentations of prejudice.

We submit this to the consideration of the organs of the Press of this enlightened country, which, being impartial in the questions now contested among the South American nations, and knowing their respective antecedents and tendencies, whatever their form of government, will be willing, as heretofore, to espouse the cause of humanity and of the civilization, so much needed on this continent.

It would be well if the American nations, instead of making such demonstrations as those to which we have referred, would, as Mr. J. B. Calojeras, an eminent Brazilian writer, proposes, agree upon some general principles which would contribute to the development of their general strength and prosperity.

The representatives of the American nations would unite in a common agreement on the principles of nationality; in cases of private international law ; in cases where difficulties between two or more American nations exist, such cases could be referred to the arbitrament of a third American power, for the avoidance of war; and all other questions of a similar nature.

It would also be much more convenient and useful to have a cordial understanding between themselves with regard to the means of promoting the increase of the population in their immense, fertile, but uninhabited territories; and facilitating the direct communications between the same countries.

The good understanding between the States of America can also be considered from a higher standpoint.

Europe, properly speaking, forms but one part in the world, it is a geographical division, and nothing more; it is not a political entity.

It seems, however, that this name means something more; that there is a certain moral consolidation between all the European nations.

Many attempts have been made to give a body and physical force to this purely moral entity.

The Universal Monarchy of Charles V. being a failure, as was also the predominance of the French Revolution, the Holy Alliance became the arbitrator, not only of Europe, but of the general policy.

Monroe was the first to raise his voice against this arbitrament; his was the first cry for the emancipation of America from the predomination of Europe.

The family of American nations being formed, they need a jury to direct their course in the way of peace and progress.

If the principal nations of the continent would encourage some such understanding, the Continent would reap therefrom more real adavntages than any which could result from those incessant conflicts, which daily weaken the several members.

We will also quote the words of a venerable Brazilian, who, in 1836, expressed himself as follows :

" The true greatness of America, and the development of American resources are intimately bound together. In vain do we behold the wealth which Providence has poured out on our country if we lack the energy of manhood.

" Let the increase of the population be encouraged by every means in our power, for that is the surest way to secure prosperity and peace at home, and to win respect abroad."

As regards the struggle now going on in the Southern part of South America, the facts have been entirely misrepresented.

No one can deny, however, that it was Lopez who invaded, plundered, and desolated territories belonging to the provinces of Matto-Grosso, Corrientes, and Rio Grande, without the least provocation on the part of Brazil or the Argentine Republic.

This act on the part of Lopez can only be explained by the mere ambition to obtain by force the disputed territories in the first-named of those provinces, the possession of which was guaranteed to Brazil by solemn treaties.

Fortunately, the invasion by the barbarains was repulsed, and the plunderers of Bella Vista, the assassins of J. Borja, the violators ofwomen at Corrientes were vanquished at Yataby, compelled to surrender at Uruguayana, and were driven away from the territories which they had stained with their crimes.

In this way have they called down vengeance on their country, and the hastily-organized armies of B razil and of the Argentine Confederation are now calling Lopez to account for the outrages against their countries, which could not be left unpunished.

These are the facts in their true light.

APPENDIX.

SINCE writing the above, we chanced upon the following article in the *Courrier des États Unis*, of October 24 of the present year, which contains a brief and sensible analysis of the unfounded accusations unreasonably launched against Brazil, the Argentine Republic, and the Oriental State of Uruguay, with regard to the terms of their treaty of Alliance of the 1st May, 1865.

THE PARAGUAYAN WAR.

" Several journals have made a great noise about the secret treaty entered into by Brazil, the Republic of Uruguay and the Argentine Republic, to settle the Paraguayan question by common consent; and have erroneously interpreted some of the stipulations of the said treaty. These exaggerations would deserve no notice, were it not that appearances somewhat tend to confirm them.

We propose to examine the triple alliance in detail, to show in what spirit it was drawn up, and make known its nature and true object; but, before commencing, we can affirm once for all that its stipulations, which have been quoted with more or less accuracy, have not the character which has been attributed to them, and that they cannot be rightly understood without a knowledge of the localities.

This compact and the coalition which gave it birth, had their origin, not in the ambition and spirit of conquest of the allies, but in the unjust pretensions and repeated provocations of the Dictator of Paraguay.

These pretensions actually amounted to an attempt on his part to have himself proclaimed *the protector* of the States of La Plata. In this manner he caused the rupture of the peace negociations then pending between the Governments of Montevideo and the Ministers of England, Brazil, and the Argentine Republic.

The rupture, the original cause of the war which is flooding with blood the banks of the Parana and Paraguay rivers, date from the 18th of June, 1864.

On the 12th of June, 1864, without making any declaration of war, Lopez ordered the seizure of the *Marquis d'Olinda*, a Brazilian steamer, employed as a packet-boat between Montevideo and Cubaya, capital of the Brazilian province of Matto-Grosso.

The President of this province was on board of the steamer at the time of its seizure, and, with the rest of the passengers, was thrown into prison. This outrage on the part of the Paraguayan Bismark was committed notwithstanding the presence, at Asuncion, of the resident minister from Brazil, and was a flagrant violation of international law, and of a special treaty concluded between Brazil and Paraguay in 1856.

Art. XVIII. of that treaty held the following stipulation :

" *That in case of a rupture between these two countries, citizens of one of the nations, residing on the territory of the other, should retain the right to their property, and even continue their businsss, with the full enjoyment of their liberty and industry.*

The Brazilian Minister at Asuncion remonstrated, but to no purpose.

He then demanded his passports, but they were refused to him, and it was only through the energetic assistance of the Minister of the United States, that he was enabled, fifteen days later, to make good his escape from Asuncion.

This transgression of the laws which regulate the relations

of civilized nations, certainly merited universal condemnation, still, however, the Government of the Argentine Republic, persisted in the strictest neutrality ; when, at the beginning of April, 1865, an Argentine vessel, the *Salto*, was seized at Asuncion, and some days after, on the 13th of April, five steamers of the Paraguyan squadron entered without warning into the harbor of Corrientes, and finding two Argentine steamers of war there anchored, the Paraguyans massacred the crew of one of the steamers, and seizing both carried them to Asuncion.

Such then are the facts whose grave import cannot be mistaken. And let us remember that this occurred previous to the 1st of May, 1865, the date of the treaty of alliance entered into by Brazil and the Republics of La Plata.

Does not the mere recital of these acts suffice to prove conclusively that this treaty was not drawn up by the contracting parties with the view to enlarge their territory, but solely for their legitimate defence, and to check the Algerian barbarity of the *Dey* of Paraguay.

For our part we have not waited until now to brand them as they deserve.

In the meantime let us consider the value of the assertions which form the basis of the claims of certain States which are not even neighbors of the territory of Paraguay.

What is there in common, excepting their origin, between the Republics of the Pacific and those of the Atlantic ?

It is true that when, in 1864, Peru desired the Argentine Government to join the league formed by the South American States against Spain, General Mitre declined to depart from his unvarying policy of non-intervention.

Is Peru justified on that account in entertaining any rancor toward the President of the Argentine Republic ? Be it as it may, the Peruvian Government has no call to interfere in the occurrences which transpire on the Rio de la Plata, as its interests are in no way compromised thereby.

As to Chili, its Government has been wise enough to preserve to this day the strictest neutrality.

With regard to Bolivia, her claim has received that attention which all just claims will ever receive from so impartial and enlightened a man as Mr. Rufino Elizalde, Minister of Foreign Affairs of the Argentine Republic.

As to the actual position of General Lopez, his titled panegyrists may say what they will, and they may publish bulletins of his victories as often as they please, but the public cannot help seeing that their hero is constantly losing ground. All are acquainted with the savage energy of the Dictator, and the fanatical enthusiasm of his soldiers; but, they are also too apt to overlook the immense preparations for war made by Paraguay during fourteen years, even children being forced to enlist.

On the other hand, the rapidity of travel which is enjoyed in Europe is apt to make one forget the almost insurmountable difficulties for carrying on military operations in America—such as the immense distances to be traversed ; the absence of roads; the frequent obstructions in the navigation of the rivers; and the necessity of transporting everything, even the most indispensable necessaries of life. Only our soldiers who have passed through the campaigns of Mexico will be able to understand the magnitude of these obstacles.

Shall Lopez, who has long deserved to be under the ban of the nations, mock his neighbors with impunity, as he has done successively with France, the United States, England, and Brazil ?

Because he possesses a fortress which he deems impregnable, shall he with impunity lay waste the territories that surround him ?

We shall not undertake to enumerate here the crimes which have made famous the hereditary dictatorship of both the Lopez, and shall confine ourselves to the mention of one, the most recent.

The Brazilian town of Uruguayana, situated on the left bank of the River Uruguay, had fallen into the power of a

Paraguayan division numbering 7,000 men, commanded by Colonel Estigarribia.

General Flores, after having overpowered the Paraguayan forces on the 15th of August, 1865, at Yatahy, on the right bank of the Uruguay River, then proceeded to place himself on the opposite bank, opposite Uruguayana. In September of the same year, at the moment when the signal for the assault was to be given, Estigarribia, the Colonel of the Paraguan forces, finding himself before a force greatly superior to his own, thought the best thing he could do was to surrender.

He was treated by General Flores with all the respect due to his rank and his misfortune, and was sent to Rio de Janeiro, where he was allowed full liberty in the city.

As usual in such cases, Lopez did not fail to wreak his vengeance on the family of Estigarribia; the mother and sister of the Colonel, the latter aged only eighteen, were given up to the brutality of Lopez soldiers, and then thrown into prison.

The sufferings of our citizens established in the States of La Plata, and the interruption of business by this dreadful war, are also urged as so many arguments against the Allies and in favor of Lopez.

But in fact Lopez has been the sole instigator of the war, and it has not been in the power of the Allies to avert it.— And now let us ask, are they not performing a sacred duty, are they not defending civilization itself, in pursuing the end which they have resolved on : the overthrow of a Government which offers no guarantee to its neighbors, no security to its commerce?

As for the fortress of Humaita, after its armament was completed, did not Lopez refuse to the European Governments the renewal of the treaty which secured the free navigation of those rivers ? Is it not, then, necessary that this fortress should be levelled to the ground, since it is a perpetual menace against the order and liberty established in the other States of La Plata ?"

Is it not, then, to the true interests of our citizens there resident to have a lasting peace secured to those countries, instead of the false and hypocritical peace which Lopez, accustomed to treachery and the utter disregard of treaties, would not fail to violate at the very first opportunity?

Our readers will find a more complete analysis in the *Journal of Commerce* of Rio de Janeiro, with regard to the protest made against the tenor of the said treaty, by the Government of Peru to the Governments of the Allied Powers, through Mr. D. Benigno G. Vigil, accredited towards them as Charge d'Affaires.

We call the attention of our readers to this exposition, made with all due calmness and carefulness, which contains the true explanation of the sole meaning and design of the stipulations of the said treaty.

PROTEST OF THE GOVERNMENT OF PERU AGAINST THE TREATY OF THE TRIPLE ALLIANCE FORMED TO CARRY ON THE WAR PROVOKED BY PARAGUAY.

I.

The *Nacional* of Buenos Ayres, of August 18, publishes the despatch addressed on the 9th of the preceding month, by the Minister of Foreign Affairs of the Republic of Peru, to the Peruvian diplomatic agent accredited towards the Argentine Republic, Paraguay and Brazil, to protest before the governments of those States against the treaty of alliance formed by them with the common object of carrying on the war to which they have been so unexpectedly provoked by the despot who oppresses the Republic of Paraguay, the integrity and independence of which, according to the Government of Peru, are threatened by the provisions of the said treaty.

We know not whether the Imperial Government has as yet received the notification contained in the despatch to which we refer, neither have we any idea as to what reception it will meet with in the councils of the crown. However, since this document has been made public by the Argentine press, the press of Brazil would be false to patriotism and to duty were it to allow it to pass unnoticed, for that document is nothing but a mass of mistaken opinions, unfounded fears, and exaggerated pretensions, as we shall endeavor to show, with all calmness and impartiality, in the brief analysis to which we shall here subject it.

The protest of Peru is made against a treaty which has not been officially published, and whose nature and design was not known even to those who gave it the irregular publicity referred to in said protest.

That a document whose authenticity is not officially established should be taken as the ground for an act which is likely to be productive of serious international difficulties, shows, to say the least, a strange disregard of prudence, and a want of the calm judgment which should be employed in matters of such grave importance.

The condition of secrecy being attached to the treaty formed between the Empire of Brazil, the Argentine Republic, and the Oriental Republic of Uruguay, it is evident that neither the Government of Peru, nor that of any other power outside of the Alliance, had the right to demand explanations thereon, or even to ask to be made officially acquainted with the whole of the said treaty, the only ones capable of judging of the utility and conveniences of that secrecy being its authors.

But granting, for the sake of argument, that this unofficial acquaintance with the document in question did really awaken such serious apprehensions in the Government of Peru, with regard to Paraguay, as to impel it to ask from the allied powers such explanations as might serve to remove those apprehensions, were the means which it had recourse to the most proper and effective ?

The Government of Peru and the allies in whose name it also speaks, were on good and friendly terms with the Empire and the Republics of La Plata. Under these circumstances, then, what would have been the most natural and proper course ?

Decidedly, if real apprehensions were excited by the treaty of alliance formed by those States to repel the aggressions of Paraguay and prevent their repetition in the future, the most natural and proper course for the Government of Peru would have been to address the allied Governments privately, as is customary and indispensable, asking for such explanations as it should deem fit and necessary.

And we are convinced that, if the Government of Peru had proceeded in this manner, as it ought certainly to have done, unless it purposely seeks some pretext for interfering in the war treacherously provoked and barbarously commenced by the Paraguayan despot, the Governments of Brazil and of the States of La Plata, would not hesitate to give the explanations which can be asked and given between friends and equals, without detriment to their personal rights and dignity. And unless a conflict has been purposely sought, all difficulty would be impossible, as the allies do not entertain nor is it possible for them to entertain any designs against the independence and integrity of Paraguay.

The present minister of Brazil, specially appointed to the States of La Plata, on entering upon his mission in the Oriental State of Uruguay, and presenting his credentials to the Chief of that Republic, gave utterance to the following eloquent and significant words :

" With her immense area, all-sufficient for her future destiny and present activity, Brazil does not cast covetous eyes on the adjoining Republics, nor does she aspire to a political supremacy which would destroy their sovereignity and liberty. A disinterested and sincere friend to *all* the South American nationalities, her truest wish is that they shall prosper and have such a sense of dignity as shall preserve them from subjection to any despotism."

Such were the words of one of the signers of the treaty of alliance, and some months later, Mr. Andrés Lemas, representative of another of the parties to the said treaty, on pre-

senting his credentials to H. M. the Emperor, in Rio de
Janeiro, proclaimed, in that solemn act, the independence and
integrity of *all* the existing nationalities as the basis of future
peace in those regions.

And shall not these proofs be accepted as evidence that the
treaty of alliance was meant and understood by the contracting parties in such a manner as not to interfere with the independence and integrity of Paraguay?

We have already said, and now repeat, that if private explanations had been asked, such as can be asked and given
between friends, all apprehensions that might really have existed would have been put to flight ; all difficulty would have
been avoided.

But alas ! the Peruvian Government has not chosen to be
guided by the dictates of prudence and calm deliberation.

Founding its complaints on a document of whose authenticity and *entireness* it could not be certain, and refraining
from all previous examination or explanation, it rashly issued
its protest against the Allied Powers.

Once launched upon this course the Peruvian Cabinet, in
order to justify its act, openly constituted itself a *judge* of the
private interests of sovereign and independent States ! And
not satisfied with the rôle, as it would be thereby confined
to the letter of the treaty, it has also assumed'the character
of *advocate* for one of the parties, and in accordance with
that character it distorts the meaning of the stipulations of
the treaty ; and again takes them, thus distorted, and con-
stituting itself the judge, condemns them !

Let us now make a brief examination of the grounds of the
accusation and give them a fair judgment.

IS THE TREATY SECRET ?

The Peruvian Government says that it is allowable to keep
treaties secret until the time of their execution, but that they
are *always* published as soon as the object of the alliance
commences to have effect.

This assertion is totally unfounded : history furnishes numerous examples to prove the contrary.

The *only judges* as to the time or opportunity of publishing a secret agreement, are the contracting parties themselves, as their convenience, their interests and their security are the things therein at stake.

Were this otherwise the equality and independence of nations could not exist.

The Peruvian Cabinet in volunteering the notoriously false assertion that secret treaties of alliance are *always* published as soon as their object commences to have effect, establishes an entirely new doctrine aggressive to the sovereignty of the nations, and tending to deprive them of their sovereign right to secure their interests and safety through secret diplomatic arrangements.

Only recently has the existence of an alliance between Italy and Prussia against Austria become known, and been subsequently officially acknowledged.

Even *after* the object of the alliance *commenced to have effect* the treaty was not published.

The ends of the alliance were consumated, Austria submitted to her expulsion from Germany and to the payment of the expenses of the war, and even then the treaty was not published ! And what is more, Europe, whose equilibrium was in question, did not demand the publication of the treaty; evidently because Europe respects the right acted upon by Prussia and Italy.

This is international law as it has been recognized and acted upon up to the present day. Even should the Peruvian Cabinet succeed in altering it, which it could not do without the consent of all the other nations, the *new law* could not have a retroactive effect and it would still be undeniable that the allies against Paraguay, in stipulating and maintaining secresy in their agreement, only acted upon a perfect and unquestionable right which the government of Peru cannot pretend to deny to them without offending their sovereignty.

The dispatch which we are now examining says that, although the treaty of the triple alliance stipulates and respects the independence and integrity of Paraguay, it nevertheless attacks them in several ways :

Firstly—In the declaration that the war is waged against the Government, and not against the people of Paraguay.

Now, in answer to this, we must call attention to the fact that one of the chief circumstances which have lessened the evils of war, is this very tendency to make a *distinction* between the government and the people.

In fact, if the governments of the Pacific, in the actual contests with Spain, had been inspired with this humane tendency, as it were so much to be desired, it is beyond all doubt that the war would not have assumed its present deplorable character.

How, let us ask, could the peaceful and industrious Spaniards, there established, be responsible for the acts of the Government of Madrid ?

Yet we Americans must acknowledge with pain that those unfortunate Spaniards, though totally innocent of the acts of their government, were imprisoned, expelled from the country, and ruined, although in their ruin that of hundreds of American families were involved.

Unfortunately the government did not choose to make the needed distinction, and consequently cannot escape the charge of having been guilty of the most unjustifiable and wanton barbarity.

The distinction of which we speak, frequently employed in all ages, has always mitigated the horrors of war, and has never caused the destruction of any nationality whatever.

In order not to weary the reader's attention by a vain display of historical facts, we shall quote only a few examples. We shall not speak of Europe save only to allude to the instance of Napoleon I., when, as all know, Europe declared against him, leaving France in the full enjoyment of her independence.

Let us take our examples from America.

In the famous struggle with the tyrant Rosas, Uruguay, France, England and, finally Brazil, made a *distinction* between the Argentine people and their tyrant.

All the manifestoes and treaties of that war invariably stipulated—*war* against the tyrant—*alliance* with the people which he oppressed.

This is precisely the *distinction* which is now made, and if possible with greater reason, in the treaty of the triple alliance against Paraguay.

If it is true, as the Government of Peru asserts, that that distinction destroys the principles of national sovereignty on which the American States are founded, why was it never protested against on the different occasions on which it was established by different powers, and in different forms, in the lengthy struggle against Rosas? Why was it, on the contrary, tacitly admitted? Why did Bolivia accept it explicitly on accepting the war declared against her by Rosas?

The Peruvian Government pretends that this distinction tends essentially and necessarily to destroy the sovereignty of nations; will it assert that it has destroyed the independence, the sovereignty, or the liberty of the Argentine people?

Let us add, however, a more direct example, which without doubt will be more conclusive for the Government of Peru.

The Peru-Bolivian Confederation being formed by General Santa Cruz, Chili declared war—against whom?—and for what end?

Making a *distinction* between the government and the people, she declared war against the protector, Santa Cruz, with the *express* end of destroying the confederation formed between Peru and Bolivia.

Chili was not embarrased by the consideration of allowing room for the will of the people of those two countries. While declaring the existence of that confederation opposed to her own safety, at the same time imposed no further restriction on the will of those people than what was needed to secure that safe-

ty ; and it even appears probable that if those people had
had the power, they would by their own choice have brought
about the new order of things thus established.

Chili then triumphed, as is well known, and Peru and
Bolivia admitted the doctrine which they now condemn; and
they not only admitted it but even went beyond it most
shamefully.

Géneral Santa Cruz being retained as a prisoner in Chili,
an agreement was formed by Chili, Peru and Bolivia, on the
7th of October, 1845, upon *the disposal of his person.*

In the preamble to the agreement are the following words:
" The governments of Chili, Bolivia and Peru *in the exer-*
cise of their right to secure the safety of the respective coun-
tries, so long disturbed by the attempts of Don Andrés
Santa Cruz to kindle civil wars, &c., &c., have agreed on the
following articles :

ART. I. Don Andrés Santa Cruz shall immediately leave
this country for Europe, where he shall remain six years,
dating from the day of his departure for a European port ;
and during that time he shall not return to any part of South
America *without the unanimous consent of the three govern-*
ments of Chili, Bolivia and Peru."

It is here evidently proved that Chili, Bolivia and Peru
made a *distinction* between the government and the people ;
that the end of that war was to *overthrow* the government
and proscribe General Santa Cruz ; and even after his overthrow and banishment those republics judged that their right
of *securing their own safety* authorized them to dispose of
the General's person, and accordingly did dispose thereof.
, And they so disposed, that even if the people of Bolivia
should desire again to entrust their government to General
Santa Cruz, such a desire was rendered of no effect, before-
hand, by the will of Chili and of Peru.

How is it then, that the Peruvian Cabinet wonders at, and
condemns the *distinction* which it has so freely employed
whenever its own interests were concerned ?

General Santa Cruz, that noble soldier of South Americau independence, was forbidden to return to any part of South America without the unanimous consent of Chili, Bolivia and Peru. This Bolivian statesman could not return to the service of his country, even had she recalled him, without the consent of the other two parties to the agreement.

And can it be possible that those who carried to such an extreme the right of securing their own safety, are the very ones who now protest against the moderate exercise of that right against the Dictator of Paraguay, who, by his barbarity and treachery in kindling the war, has forfeited all claim on the protection of international law and the general custom of civilized nations ?

In Paraguay the only real entity is the Dictator; he alone thinks ; he alone speaks ; he alone acts.

The people, in time of peace, is a mere machine for producing the wealth of the lord of the land ; in time of war it is simply a destructive engine controlled by the all-powerful will of the Dictator.

Even if the *distinction* between governments and the people had never existed before, it would certainly have to be exercised now in the question of Paraguay and her downtrodden people. That *distinction* would be inevitable.

In vain does the Peruvian protest speak of the *will* of the Paraguayan people, of the *constitution* of Paraguay.

The whole world knows that in Paraguay there is but one will, and but one constitution : the will and the absolute power of the Lopez family.

The chief of that family exercises omnipotence.

He then, is the only one responsible in Paraguay, for he is the only one who resolves and acts.

It being thus demonstrated, afd even with the authority of the example furnished by Chili, Peru and Bolivia, that the allies only exercised a legitimate right in determining on the downfall of a dictator whose power is irreconcilable with the peace and safety of their respective countries, the next thing which presents itself after the fall of the present government is the necessity of substituting it by another one.

Who is to make this substitution ?

That is what we shall consider in another article, continuing our analysis of the Peruvian protest. To-day we shall proceed no further, so as not to weary the reader's attention.

II.

Who ought to substitute the Government of the Republic of Paraguay, which the triple-alliance is endeavoring to over-throw ?

This was the question with which we ended the first article that we wrote on the Peruvian protest, the analysis of which we are going to continue to-day. Since the nationality of Paraguay is recognized, it is clear that the Paraguayan people, called to political life by the victory of the alliance, is the one which ought to choose the new government.

In this recognition of the right of a liberated nation to adopt the institutions which may suit her, and select its own government, the Peruvian Cabinet descry a new attack on the autonomy of Paraguay.

But what is it that Peru wants to be done ?

Does she want that the dictatorship should be made heriditary, and that the supreme power should be rendered transmissible like a fiducial family inheritance ?

Does she want to deny the Paraguayan nation the right of legislating, and of organizing the public authorities which ought to govern the country ?

In case the stipulations of the treaty were not carried into effect, and the government of Lopez should be overthrown, there would be no other remedy than to give the people of Paraguay a government.

Is it thus that Peru understands the autonomy of the Paraguayan people ?

The declaration that the said people shall choose for themselves the institutions and government of which they approve, is nevertheless the second innovation of which the powers who signed the treaty of the Triple-Alliance are guilty.

The other innovations which are revolting to the conscience of Americans are the following :

1° To guarantee collectively, for five years, to Paraguay her sovereignty, independence, and territorial integrity.

2° To establish the bases of the adjustment of the future boundaries with Paraguay.

3° That the fortress of Humaitá shall be razed to the ground, and that no other fortresses of the same kind shall be constructed; also, that the arms and ammunition found in Paraguay shall be divided among the allied powers.

In order to fully understand well these stipulations, it will be necessary to explain the social, political and geographical position of Paraguay.

The said nation has never governed itself; from a colony it passed without transition to the dictatorship of Dr. Francia, whose administration is to this day continued by his successors.

The people is a nation of passive serfs, who possess nothing of their own, who work for the owner of the soil, who fight and die without knowing for whom or for what, when the owner orders them to do so.

They have no men who are fit to be administrators, and are ignorant of their own rights, as well as of all the ideas which prevail in the present century. They merely understand to obey, to do what they are told to do with arms in hand, *and to hate foreigners.*

The Dictator has made every man a soldier. In civilized societies the tribute of blood has its limits, yet Lopez has dragged the whole of the population to the battlefield. This unheard of circumstance may have a result without precedence in the present century, if the war should be prolonged, viz., the annihilation of the whole of the male population of Paraguay.

These simple indications are sufficient to portray what may be the position of Paraguay when Lopez falls.

Suppose it were the sinister intention of the victors to absorb that nationality, they could easily do so as soon as they have achieved their victory. All that they would have to do would be to substitute their own authority for the former, and keep the people under the subjugation to which they are accustomed.

But, fortunately for the people of Paraguay, as well as for the international peace of her neighbors, Providence, in blinding Lopez, as he blinds every one destined to fall, made him constantly offend his three immediate neighbors, and was himself the instigator of that triple alliance which will put an end to his barbarous and agressive tyranny.

That league or alliance, created by Lopez, is the best guarantee for the autonomy of Paraguay, even if no other were sufficient.

Brazil can never sanction the absorption of Paraguay by the Argentine Republic, nor can the latter permit Brazil to absorb Paraguay. The Oriental State, situated between Brazil and the Argentine Republic, is relatively weak, and to her the agrandizement or disequilibrium of her neighbors cannot be favorable, nor can she be favorable to the doctrines that " might is right," and that the stronger nationalities should be permitted to divide the smaller ones among themselves.

These different interests will evidently serve as a bond of unity and friendship between the allied powers, and at the same time make them respect the autonomy and territorial integrity of Paraguay.

If, therefore, the nationality of the said country remains intact, the victory of the allied powers will confer on it the conditions of a free people.

This would no doubt be a great change for the people of Paraguay. It is natural that such a sudden and absolute transition would be productive of intestine agitations and difficulties. It would doubtless be a hard and perilous apprenticeship, which the people of Paraguay would have to serve at their own cost.

In order that those internal difficulties should not destroy the Paraguayan nationality, by discouraging and causing her to solicit or accept a protectorate which should affect the same, the treaty guaranteed, for five years, the independence and territorial integrity of the country.

The said guarantee is "collective," which means to say, that, as the interests of the Allies neither permit them to annihilate nor dismember Paraguay, the guarantee is perfectly sincere and efficacious. It is true that the Allies might have omitted to give the said guarantees; but, if they did not give it, Paraguay would remain exposed, in her autonomy as well in her territorial integrity, to all the perils in which her social and political condition might place her; she would also be exposed to the extenuation in which the war would leave her, and the preponderance which the victory would give to Brazil as well as to the Argentine Republic. The treaty protects her from those perils, and guarantees her autonomy and integrity. And is it against such a guarantee that the Peruvian cabinet protests?

If the Allies had not been sincere in their desire to save the Paraguayan nationality, they might have omitted this point in the treaty; and each of the allied powers might have reserved to itself liberty of action to absorb or neutralize the conquered Republic, or to dispute the possession of her amongst themselves on the day of victory.

Would Peru have been satisfied with such proceedings?

The guarantee is limited to five years; and this is another chapter in the accusations of the Peruvian cabinet.

From the circumstance that the guarantee is limited to such a period, the aforesaid cabinet draws the conclusion that any of the Allies or all of them together have the intention of absorbing Paraguay.

We are almost loth to answer such a supposition.

If they had the intention of absorbing Paraguay, *especially if the three allied powers intended to do so jointly*, as the Peruvian Government appears to think, it must be confessed that the negotiators of the treaty of the Triple-Alliance have made a sad mistake.

Why should they then renounce the favorable moment, when the victory had been achieved, and protect Paraguay during five years, thus giving her sufficient time not only to get safely out of the many dangers which beset her, but also to organize and strengthen her government, recover her forces lost during the war, while she would also have learned to love and defend her autonomy.

The Allies do not wish to behold Paraguay disorganized and conquered; they will postpone making their claims until she has recovered her wasted strength, and is able to defend herself properly and by the help of such natural allies on whom she may reckon. This is one of the most startling revelations contained in the Peruvian protest.

The same loyal thought which inspired the collective guarantee, as already explained, inspired also the bases for adjusting the boundaries. Paraguay is litigating with Brazil and the Argentine Republic about her boundaries. It would therefore be natural to settle this matter as soon as peace should be concluded, arranging at the same time the other pending questions.

If Paraguay were once conquered, it would hardly be able to dispute the pretensions of the victors; and these pretensions might be of such a nature that they cancelled totally, and in its most important consequences, the guarantee granted to the autonomy and integrity of the Republic.

In what manner would it be possible to resist the dangers which once threatened Paraguay, and also the future peace of all those countries? It can, certainly, only be done by restraining at once the ambition which the victory might inspire.

And the only practical means of arriving at such a beneficial and important result would be, no doubt, to impose no other boundaries on the conquered republic of Paraguay than those which were proposed to her in the negotiations previous to the war, when she was yet intact and strong.

And this, only this, is what the Triple-Alliance wanted to do; but Peru condemns it!

Would the Peruvian cabinet prefer that the sword of the conquerors should trace the boundaries of conquered Paraguay according to their own fancy?

If this point had also been omitted in the treaty, and Paraguay had been exposed to be parcelled out, on pretext of adjusting the boundaries, perhaps, then, the Peruvian cabinet might have remained silent on that subject.

The adjustment of boundaries are naturally perpetual, and consequently the guarantee which the Allies give to them is equally so.

 · If the Peruvian Government were not inclined to condemn everything, it would have seen that the 17th article, which solely has reference to a permanent adjustment, is calculated to avoid the recommencement of a war from want of faith in the adjustments which the peace might have been productive of.

The fortress of Humaitá, and others of the same nature (and these are the only ones which have been mentioned), is and would be a threat and an obstacle to the free navigation of the rivers, owing to its position and all its qualities.

The right of navigating in those rivers rests (let us use the words pronounced by the United States Government) on a principle profoundly engraved on the human mind, viz., that the ocean is open to all men, and that the rivers are equally so to all river navigators.

The justice of this natural right was recognized and sanctioned by Paraguay herself in favor of her population and her neighbors, on the banks of her rivers; and at the solicitation of Brazil and of the Argentine Republics, this right was extended to all other nations, and in such terms that it was understood, and with good reason too, that the conditions in which the treaties placed the free navigation of the river La Plata, and its great tributaries, made it equal to the ocean.

The paragraph in the treaty which orders the demolition of such fortresses is therefore a liberal measure which interests all nations, Paraguay included, whose commercial progress and government revenue are increased thereby, while it gives to the empire of Brazil the right of communication, by river, with her province of Matto Grosso.

Humaitá was a barrier in the common road, to the gate of which she herself only had the key. From this many difficulties arose, which more than once imperilled the peace of those nations. Even if Humaitá had not been a menace to the safety of the neighboring territories, even if it had not been a nest of refuge to all the birds of prey which devastate the province of Corrientes, even if painful experience had not proved to us that such a fortress (able to contain a whole army) was a source of constant danger to the neighboring countries, who were obliged to be on a war footing in times of peace; it sufficed that it was an obstacle to free navigation, and it ought therefore to be demolished and never permitted to be erected again.

The Argentine and Oriental Republics spontaneously admitted the doctrine that the island of Martin Garcia could not be an embarrassment to the free navigation, and, therefore, they at once agreed that the said island *should remain neutral in time of war*, and what is more, that it should appertain in common to the fiscal offices of the people dwelling on the banks of the rivers.

This is the principle established in the treaties of the Brazilian Empire and the Argentine Republics with Paraguay herself, as well as with England, France, the United States, Italy, &c.

As far as regards the arms and ammunitions, the treaty only says that those which were found should be divided amongst the conquerors. They had earned those with their own blood, and, unfortunately, they had cost them dearly. For what reason should the Peruvian cabinet deny the Allies the legitimate possession of the arms which they had wrested from the hands of their enemies in an open and loyal war?

But there was one weighty reason besides which justified such a measure. It could never suit the Allies to lay aside at once their own arms, and to leave in the hands of their fanatic and half-savage enemies an immense quantity of arms and ammunition, collected during a period of twenty years, in order to rush at once and unexpectedly, like a terrible avalanche, on their neighbors. Such a measure would have been contrary and dangerous to the commercial, industrial and social interests of the Allies, as well as to those of other nations.

But by disposing at once of all those elements of war which had been legitimately won, all those countries might be enabled, without much delay, to return to peaceful occupations.

This does not imply, as the Peruvian protest gratuitously observes, that Paraguay should not be permitted to have a military force, to preserve order at home, and defend her against her enemies; because, in fully recognizing her autonomy, one must, of course, at the same time, recognize her right to have such an armed force as she may consider requisite.

She has one *already*, and the Allies, in accordance with their own principles, will agree to her keeping it, and will not in future put any difficulties in the way of the Paraguayan Government to prevent it from exercising this right, which, as a sovereign and independent State, she can do at her own will, without limits. Brazil, as well as the Argentine Republic and Oriental State, do not have any other aim; nor have they any other interest at heart than that of having for a neighbor a well-organized State, which is governed in accordance with the civilized doctrines now in general use— a State which respects herself, and also knows how to respect the legitimate rights and interests of her neighbors.

But Brazil, the Argentine and Oriental Republics, will not and cannot suffer to be continually menaced by the capricious will of a despot, who governs at his own pleasure a people which he oppresses and keeps in subjugation.

Let Paraguay regenerate herself, and enter into the enjoyment of a free system of government, which, in guaranteeing her own rights, also guarantees those of Brazil, the Argentine Republic, and the Oriental State, giving to all those countries the tranquility which they need for the progressive development of their prosperity and greatness.

We have now finished the analysis which we intended to make of the Peruvian protest. It now remains for us to offer to the readers a few general observations on the causes which we presume have induced the Peruvian Cabinet to act in this unexpected manner.

This matter will be the subject of our third and last article.

III.

In the foregoing paragraphs we have analyzed, one by one, all the accusations made by the Peruvian Government in their protest against the treaty of the triple alliance; and how the said government made that protest disdaining all amicable explanations.

From our analysis it may be seen that if the Government of Peru had cared to proceed in a proper manner, it might easily have obtained such explanations and assurances as would at once have satisfied its own scruples and the scruples of the *American people*, of which it has constituted itself the organ, and which it supposes to be alarmed.

But the fact is that the Peruvian Cabinet does not really seek explanations; what it seeks is a quarrel.

It is well known that Chili, Peru and Bolivia desired that all America together should make common cause in their war against Spain, a war which possibly might have been avoided; and that they desired, especially Chili, that the Argentine Republics should espouse their cause.

If these Republics had acceded to the request of Chili,

their position in the Atlantic would have made them the theatre of a war, to which they had not in the least contributed, and in which none of their interests were concerned.

Chili, who counted upon having the said war endorsed, (may this expression be permitted to us) by the Republics of La Plata, was deeply offended because the Republics, not only refused to do so, but rejected the principle of antagonism which Chili endeavored to establish as a doctrine and a fact between Europe and America.

From that time Chili and her allies have sought to come in contact with the defeated parties of the States of La Plata ; and from that contact have imbibed the illusions cherished by all such parties.

Confounding the difficulties which the triple-alliance encountered in the topography of Paraguay, with the preponderance of Lopez in the actual war, they believed that by giving moral support to Paraguay, and thus encouraging the defeated parties of the States of La Plata, and inciting them to a revolution, they might succeed in nullifying the alliance, and save Paraguay who, naturally adheres to the antagonism against Europe.

The nullification of the alliance would satisfy their pride, and while they dreamed of the possibility that the Republics of the La Plata might yet side with them in their war against Spain, (from which these wanted to keep clear) those apostles of Americanism were flattered by the prospect of territorial, á la Rosas, aggrandizement.

Thus Chili was to have Argentine Patagonia which already figures on her maps under the name of Oriental Chili. .

Peru dreamt of cancelling her boundary-treaty with Brazil and of extending her possessions in the Amazon regions; and Bolivia of extending hers at the cost of Paraguay, of the Argentine Republics and of Brazil.

This plan would indeed be a magnificent one, were it not founded on delusion. The basis is faulty, viz : that Paraguay is to triumph in the present war over the armies of the triple-alliance.

But such dreams and delusions are of no use. Neither Chili nor Peru can command these seas, and none of their men-of-war will disturb the triple-alliance.

The war in which Chili and Peru are engaged with Spain, their troubles at home, and their financial position, will not permit them to earry on a war with us by land.

The only kind of hostility which they can show towards us, is by giving moral support to Lopez, and by animating the defeated parties in the Republics of La Plata.

This hostility exists already ; the protest shows it.

It was for this reason that the Peruvian Cabinet did not seek any previous explanations, it was for this reason that putting all consideration aside, it published the protest before it had been delivered to the governments to which it was directed ; and, therefore, the said protest is nothing more than an inconsiderate reproduction of the press of Lopez.

For instance, the *America*, (mouth-piece of the Paraguayan Dictator in the States of La Plata) stated in its number of the 13th May ultimo, that the treaty of the triple-alliance had decreed the partition of the *American Poland*, and the Peruvian Cabinet, which in the protest aforementioned, does nothing but support the malignant suggestions and suppositions of the Lopez press, repeats seriously that, to reduce Paraguay to an *American Poland*, would be a disgrace, which America could not witness without covering herself with shame.

We, therefore, repeat that the Peruvian protest is neither in fact, nor in form, a diplomatic document. It is purely and simply *hostility*. All that can be said in reply to it is this : What right have you to judge of the actions of sovereign and independent States, who are only exercising their lawful rights in the defence of their own safety, and of their legitimate and indisputable interests, without offending yours.

Do you claim to be the personification of America, of that immense region divided into so many different States, each so perfectly independent of the others ? Is not that personi-

52

fication of America which you arrogate to yourself, an usurpation for which you have not even a pretext?

We do not acknowledge that personification, and we reject the international policy which you pretend to establish. We do so because your object is to make a Continental American war out of a war which exists only between an American and an European power, or between two or more American States.

We regret it also because you would thus create a spirit of permanent animosity between Europe and America.

The war with Spain in which you are engaged, you call, even in the protest of which we have been speaking, *war with Europe!* Alliance for repelling the violent attacks and arrogant pretensions of *Europe!*

We consider that league of yours against Europe detrimental to the most important and essential interests of America, who receives from the old world laborers, capital, and all the benefits of its commerce, industry and scientific development.

We are resolved to be independent, yes, but not only of Europe, but also of all American nations, whatever their names—be they Chile, Peru, or Bolivia.

We exact from the European nations only what we exact from the American nations, that our absolute and perfect independence be respected.

That American league of yours will never be completed, because it is an insensate idea.

If such a league were established, it would create a European league against America.

You are decidedly compromising the most essential interests of America, and calling forth perils which did not exist before. Because we cannot join you in your mad course, you turn against us, but you are at the same time deceiving yourselves.

You cannot save Lopez. The allied armies will overthrow his power. You may perhaps create some disturbance on the frontiers, but in such case, you will not escape from the responsibility which may result therefrom.

In conclusion, we sincerely desire to remain in peace with you. To accomplish this, you have merely to remain tranquil and neutral, which you ought to do, considering that none of your legitimate rights or interests have been attacked.

Rio de Janeiro, 14th September, 1866.

With respect to the note of His Excellency, Señor Taborga, Minister of Foreign Relations of the Republic of Bolivia, we shall confine ourselves to reproducing, in the following documents, the notes which were addressed to him, in answer, by the Governments of the Argentine Republic, and of His Majesty the Emperor of Brazil :

NOTE OF THE GOVERNMENT OF BRAZIL TO THAT OF THE REPUBLIC OF BOLIVIA.

{ Office of Foreign Affairs,
{ Rio de Janeiro, Sept. 15, 1866.

His Excellency, Don José R. Taborga, Minister of Foreign Relations of Bolivia, in a note dated July 6th, of the present year, whose receipt I hereby acknowledge, asks, by order of His Excellency, the provisional President, that the Government of Brazil shall declare the genuineness or falsity of the text of a treaty of alliance which has been made public through the press, said to be formed between Brazil, the Argentine Republic and Uruguay.

The Bolivian Government thus addresses the Government of Brazil, because one of the articles of that treaty contains certain stipulations concerning boundaries, which appear to deprive Bolivia of territory, which she claims, on the right bank of the Paraguay.

In answering Mr. Taborgas, by order of His Majesty the Emperor, to whom the said note was presented, I shall confine myself to a brief declaration, which cannot fail to satisfy the Government of Bolivia, as it will show how carefully the allies have avoided anything, in their agreements, which might injure a friendly nation.

His Majesty's Government cannot make any declaration
as to the genuineness or falsity of the treaty which came to
the knowledge of His Excellency, the President, as it has
bound itself to preserve the secresy of the treaties formed
with its allies; but it can and does declare that those treaties
not only respect all rights which Bolivia may have in any
part of the territory on the right bank of the Paraguay, but
also expressly mentions them.

The boundaries between Brazil and Bolivia are not yet
determined on. This question, which has nothing to do with
the Paraguayan war, and which we shall not attempt to discuss on this occasion, cannot and does not receive any detriment from any of the stipulations of alliance.

The Imperial Government, I repeat, respects that question
and hopes that it will be speedily settled; and for its part
will do everything in its power to bring about an agreement
which shall satisfy both countries.

I have the honor to offer to your Excellency the assurances
of my highest esteem and most distinguished consideration.

MARTIM FRANCISCO Ribeiro DE ANDRADA.

*To His Excellency, Don José R. Taborga, Minister of For-
eign Relations of the Republic of Bolivia.*

REPLY TO THE BOLIVIAN PROTEST.

MINISTRY OF FOREIGN AFFAIRS,
BUENOS AYRES, *August* 18, 1866.

To HIS EXCELLENCY THE MINISTER OF FOREIGN AFFAIRS
OF THE REPUBLIC OF BOLIVIA:

EXCELLENCY—I have the honor of replying to your note
dated on the 6th of last July, which came to hand yesterday,
the 17th instant.

The Argentine Government was surprized by the contents
of said note, and is convinced that the Government of Bolivia will easily recognize the little foundation it had for its
alarm and consequent proceeding.

As the treaty of alliance between the Argentine, Brazilian and Oriental Governments against that of Paraguay is secret, the Argentine Government cannot enter into any discussion or consideration of its provisions, nor make any revelation with regard to its contents. Nor can the Bolivian Government appeal to said treaty, nor to any publication concerning this subject, as it stands at present, to support the idea that friendly governments are engaged in plotting to despoil the republic of Bolivia of any territory that belongs to it, under the plea of their war with Paraguay. Such a suspicion becomes the more unjustifiable and inexplicable from the fact, that the Argentine Government signed a treaty of amity, commerce, navigation and boundaries with the representative of Bolivia, on the 2d day of May, 1865—that is, on the day following the signing of the Alliance—and the Argentine Congress has authorized its ratification. In the Twentieth Article, said treaty stipulates that "the boundaries between the Argentine Republic and Bolivia shall be settled by special treaty between the two governments after a commission, to be appointed by both parties, shall have examined the respective titles, made the necessary surveys, and presented the plan or plans of the boundary line. Both Governments shall take the necessary steps to have this stipulation carried out. In the meantime, possession shall give no right to territory which shall not have belonged originally to one or the other nation."

If the ratifications of said treaty have not as yet been exchanged, the reason is that the Bolivian Chargè requested an extension of time, as appears from the protocol annexed.— But in order that the Government of Bolivia may be convinced of its error, I annex hereto copies of the notes exchanged at the time of signing the treaty of alliance between the plenipotentiaries of the Government of his Majesty the Emperor of Brazil and of the Oriental Republic of Uruguay, by which they recognized, as they were bound to do, the rights which the republic of Bolivia has to the territory lying on the right bank of the Paraguay. The treaty of alliance could have no reference whatever to a question of boundaries between the Argentine Republic and Bolivia, nor between the latter and the Empire of Brazil. I have no doubt that these explanations will give entire satisfaction to the Government of Bolivia, and that said Government will recognize therein an additional proof of the respect which the Argentine Republic has for the rights of others, especially when the Republic of Bolivia is concerned, for to it she is bound by ties of the most fraternal sympathy, and with its valuable co-operation she hopes to be able to establish and settle the peace and prosperity of both peoples upon a more solid basis. Hence, I am pleased to reiterate to your Excellency the assurances of my high and distinguished consideration.

RUFINO DE ELIZALDE.

ERRATUM.

Page.	Line.	Says:	Should say:
12,	8,	of 1st May,	of 23d Jan. 1865, between Chili, Peru, Bolivia and Ecuador.
25,	18,	1836,	1838.
28,	15,	Cubaya,	Cuyaba.
29,	6,	Paraguyan,	Paraguayan.
29,	19,	*Dey*,	Bey.
32,	23,	Paraguay,	Uruguay.
36,	23,	the war, and	the war, Italy occupying Venetia, and
37,	24,	Government did,	Government of Peru did.
48,	24,	has one *already*,	will possess one.
52,	8,	We regret,	We reject.

Wherever it may say "Argentine Republics," read Republics of La Plata.

www.ingramcontent.com/pod-product-compliance
Lightning Source LLC
Chambersburg PA
CBHW021640270326
41931CB00008B/1092